NEV[illegible] AT A BABOON

ADVENTURES OF A TEA MAN IN AFRICA

Never Throw Rocks At A Baboon

Adventures of a Tea Man in Africa

BARRY W. COOPER
International Tea Master

Published by Cooper Venture Associates.

Visit us at www.CooperTea.com

Printed in China.

Cover and interior design by The Creative Alliance
Publishing consultation by Colleen Norwine
Editing by Tara Weaver
Copy editing by Diana Miller
Maps by Scott Church Creative

ISBN-10: 0-9777397-0-8
ISBN-13: 978-0-9777397-0-7

For N.F.H. (Toby) Fleming
Mentor, Friend and Tea Man Extraordinaire.

Contents

Introduction

I AM A WHITE AFRICAN AMERICAN. I GREW UP IN KENYA, AS IDYLLIC, RAW, VIOLENT, AND BEAUTIFUL A PLACE AS THERE IS ON THIS EARTH.

When I tell people I am a White African American, a strained silence results. It sounds politically incorrect. A White African American? How could that be? Surely no such creature exists.

Well, of course we do. I suspect there are thousands of us—probably tens of thousands—scattered across America. We are the sons and daughters of the white colonies of Africa: the Southern Rhodesians; the Northern Rhodesians; the kids who grew up in Nyasaland, Tanganyika, South Africa, or Kenya. We were raised in families who spent generations on the dark continent, only to find ourselves homeless and stateless as Southern Rhodesia toppled into Zimbabwe and Northern Rhodesia became Zambia, Nyasaland became Malawi, and Tanganyika renamed itself to an almost familiar Tanzania.

All of these and many more countries were the playgrounds for a pampered race of white children, raised by black nannies and devoted to sports and club life. We banded together in comfortable groups with similar likes and dislikes. Our society signed "chits" for everything, even groceries, so that today I often find myself with no money in my pockets and being forced to use a credit card for a $2.50 purchase. We were raised to view leadership as a natural event, and mastery as a destiny. We were used to broad verandas, and wide vistas of open plains and soaring skies.

We were the sons of soldiers, farmers, diplomats, missionaries, lawyers, policemen, and civil servants. We were raised with servants, gardeners, and cooks, in homes that rambled on forever and were surrounded by English country gardens and huge lawns that were cut and clipped by an army of gardeners.

Our parents lived lives surrounded by chintz and politics and cocktail parties. Their time was spent on affairs of state—and of the more pleasurable kind. Their interests all coalesced into the single theme of maintaining their lifestyle and the British flag flying over the colony, no matter what part of Africa it happened to be.

At an early age we knew that rhinos could not see worth a damn but could hear you a mile away and were mean.

We children were raised with manners of a bygone age. We were held to behaviors and standards that, even as we were being taught them, were disappearing forever in the faraway land called England, where we would go on "home leave."

We were cultural misfits. Comfortable in our African heritage, we were at home in the wilds of Africa and attuned to where puff adders would rest, where crocodiles would slide, and how much angostura bitters it took to make a pink gin without turning it red. We were universally raised with a Gordon's gin bottle on the center of the dining room table that held filtered water that had been run though a porous rock.

At an early age we knew that rhinos could not see worth a damn but could hear you a mile away and were mean. That the lazy looking buffalo with its droopy horns and droopy looking face was by far the most dangerous animal on the plains and should never be ignored. That male lions were pussycats and would not hurt a fly, but that female lions viewed us as a meal. We knew to shake out our slippers in the morning to avoid crushing centipedes against our toes, and that earwigs could crawl into your ear if you slept on an infested pillow. We knew that Oxford and Cambridge were the only universities in the world and that God was an Englishman.

As boys we were taught the manly art of rugby and cricket and boxing. We viewed girls as desirable objects—remote, unattainable, and to be protected with your life if necessary. We knew that anyone suggesting differently was a liar. "Manners maketh the man" was not just a saying to us, it was the law. We were totally safe and secure in an entirely alien land.

We were as much at home in Kenya as the smallest toto (child) running around naked in a village. The same love of Africa runs in our blood. We were universal in our uniforms and blazers at our English schools—short shorts; striped ties; and blue, red, or green blazers. We were divided into houses at school, all bearing the names of English, Scottish, Welsh, and occasionally Irish noblemen. The names Clive, Wellington, Hawk, Frobisher, and Rhodes were familiar to us before we even opened up our history books.

We regarded them as heroes. Clive of India—a lone adventurer who conquered one of the most populated lands in the world, making it the jewel in the crown. We were being raised to that same destiny. I think we must have been interchangeable at that time. You could have taken a child out of school in Salisbury, Southern Rhodesia, whisk him or her into a school in Nairobi, Kenya, and he or she would not be noticed unless their blazer was of a different color.

We were raised to recognize a gentleman by his punctuality, the force of his personality, the tone of his voice and the bearing of his shoulders. Young district commissioners would arrive from London to take on responsibilities for administrating swathes of territory the size of southern England. No one questioned their ability or right to do so.

As historians delve into the past and write about the policies and attitudes of the times I grew up in, I see the arrogance and paternalism that was not apparent to me as a child. But I cannot quibble with the sheer joy of my childhood in Africa; politics aside, I was a child and saw things as a child.

It was a doomed society even as we were being raised in it. Our fate was to be the immigrants of a new age. We were a generation of children who were destined to be travelers, to be the storytellers of a life that was disappearing even as we were living it. We were to take with us the memories and experiences of growing up in

Africa—as white children but as native as could be—and go out into the wide world to tell our story.

After Independence we scattered like seeds in the wind. The children of the settlers had no place to settle. Kenya was my childhood home, and England is my birthplace, and America is now my homeland.

I have watched in horror as Africa has disintegrated into a morass of warlords, warfare, corruption, incompetence, malpractice, and illness. Despite all the faults that its inhabitants bring to it, the continent remains serene and magnificent, soaring above the petty vices of its rulers. It retains its ancient soul. Africa gets in your blood. Once you have experienced the inner pull of the dark continent, life can never be the same again. It tugs at your heart and brings you back.

Africa was the birthplace of mankind, it is terribly old, and its recent history of fresh new nations also makes it terribly young. Africa gave me a fractured cultural background, but one that has made me comfortable in any cultural setting.

Although I move between homes in Boulder, Colorado and St. Croix, in the U.S. Virgin Islands, I feel most at peace in St. Croix. It's an island that was populated with the seeds brought over from Africa in the Danish slave ships. Bougainvillea, thorn trees, flame trees, and hibiscus bushes overflow on the island. The scents and sights of my childhood resonate within me. When I am there, at a deep level I am home.

Barry P. W. Cooper
St. Croix, US Virgin Islands

Chapter 1
A Soldier and a Spy

I FIRST SAW A TEA BUSH IN MALAYSIA WHEN I WAS FIVE YEARS OLD. IT WAS 1949. MY FATHER, A PROFESSIONAL SOLDIER, WAS ATTACHED TO THE 7TH BATTALION OF THE GURKHA, TRAINING TROOPS ON COUNTERINSURGENCY TECHNIQUES.

My mother worked for MI6, the secret intelligence service, and was responsible for paying the informers who were used to help track down the communist terror gangs.

The British Army rest camp was in the Cameron Highlands, a verdant patch of mountaintop that was cool and misty and surrounded by tea bushes. Unfortunately, it was also surrounded by communist guerillas.

To get to the rest camp, you had to join a scheduled convoy. My father did not like convoys. "Why tell your enemy what time you are going to leave and then drive slowly past him?" I heard him tell my mother. Instead we traveled with a soldier who had a machine gun in the back of the car. The car was a black Hillman Minx. I do not think there were too many private cars in Malaya at that time, but my parents had one.

We were on holiday. My father was driving, my mother was in the front seat, and my sister and I were in the back—along with a sergeant who had a machine gun in his hands to defend us in case of an ambush. As I look back, I now think he was there to make sure my mother and father were not captured. To be killed if necessary, but not captured.

We saw a communist guerilla on the way up the mountain. He was sitting on a mile marker, a rifle in his lap. We were past him and round the corner before he moved. I remember my father accelerating the car though.

As we climbed up toward the official army rest camp perched atop the hills, we drove through rolling, verdant valleys full of these little bushes. I remember looking out and wondering how come all the bushes were the same size and how all the rows could be equidistant, and I was fascinated by the way they followed the contours of the land.

Of course I now know that contoured planting prevents runoff from the rain, and that each tea bush is the same height to allow tea pluckers to harvest the tea leaves. But to a five-year-old boy, those orderly, precise rows were a source of wonder and amazement.

My father had spent the Second World War training SOE agents in counterterrorism tactics. He worked at London's Hendon Police College. The Special Operations Executive was created by Winston Churchill in July 1940 to organize sabotage and general mayhem in occupied Europe. Father taught agents how to blow things up, dismantle railroad tracks, kill people with a single punch, and other useful day-to-day needs for an undercover agent.

He trained Germans who wanted to fight Hitler, and British and American prisoners who were given the option of a severe prison sentence or a short life as a commando. If they were killed, they received the honor of having died in action. He told me of Poles, Swiss, and all manner of men who went silently into the night, back to Europe to fight. My father lost both his brothers in the war and, like most hard men of a hard profession, he was very gentle around his family and friends.

When the war ended, communists infiltrated the Malaysian Peninsula and the British Army was sent out to repel the guerillas; my father was sent to train them. That is how I ended up in Malaya, and in Kenya five years later, for my second encounter with the tea bush.

The Mau Mau, a revolt in Kenya against British rule, began in the early 1950s, and by 1954 Kenya was a dangerous place to live. Cattle were being hamstrung, people were being killed in horrendous fashion, and a pall was being cast over a beautiful country.

Our family arrived in Kenya in March 1954. My sister and I did not feel the effects of the emergency, although we were firmly told that we had to be in the house at dusk. I slept in a room with a loft that had a steep ladder; if I heard noises or gunshots, my instructions were to take my sister and climb the ladder and pull it up behind us. We were then to sit and wait for our parents. In the loft were switches to battery-operated sirens. I was to switch on the sirens so that the neighbors would hear that we were in distress or being attacked.

I caught my second glimpse of tea bushes as we took a visit to the Limuru Brackenhurst Hotel, perched in the Highlands of Kenya, about fifteen miles outside Nairobi. I recognized the bushes immediately. Now it was certain. Gazing wide-eyed at the rolling hills, I felt a distant call that came to define my life.

My family: Roland, Susan, Sylvia and myself.

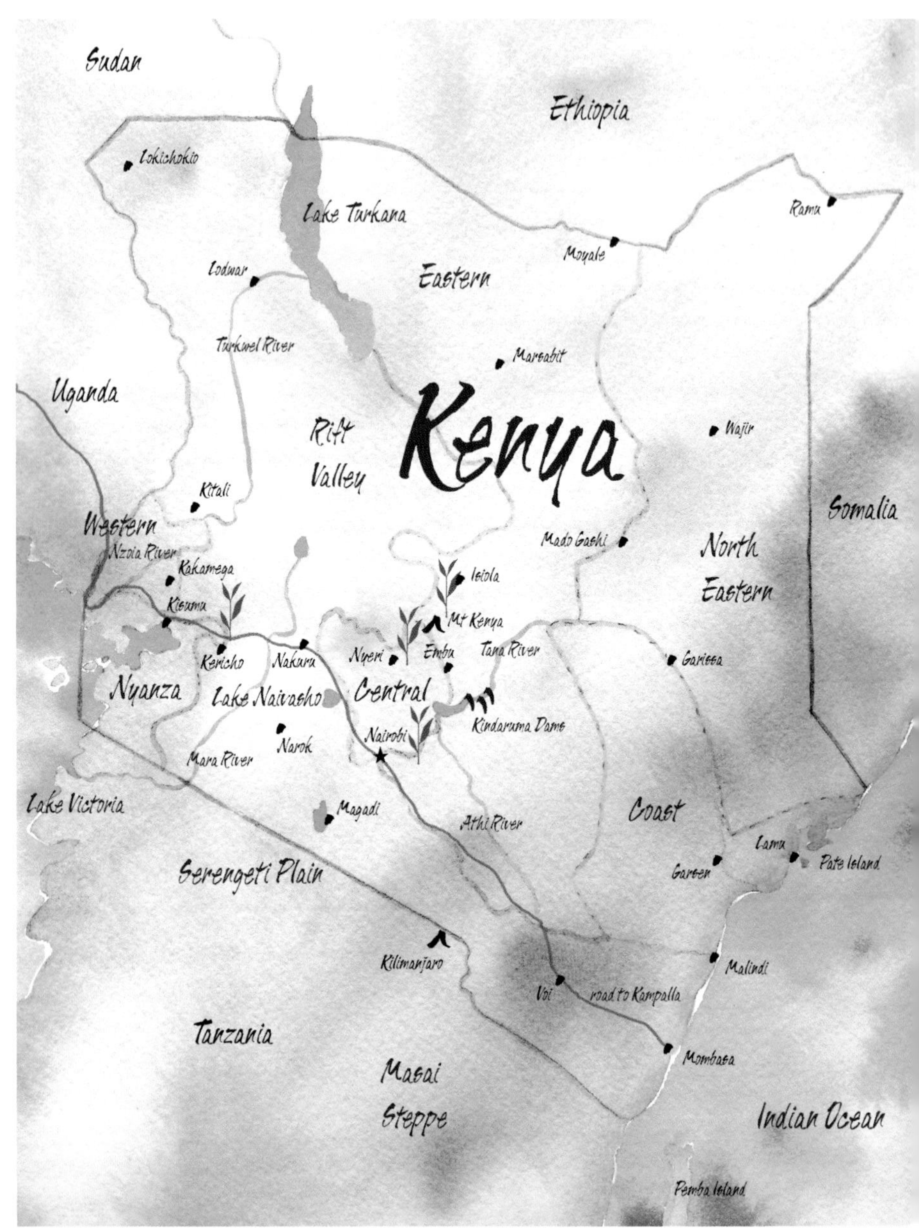
Sudan
Ethiopia
Lokichokio
Lake Turkana
Ramu
Moyale
Lodwar
Eastern
Turkwel River
Marsabit
Uganda
Kenya
Rift Valley
Wajir
Kitali
Somalia
Western
Mado Gashi
North Eastern
Nzoia River
Kakamega
Isiola
Kisumu
Mt Kenya
Tana River
Kericho
Nakuru
Nyeri
Embu
Garissa
Nyanza
Lake Naivasho
Central
Kindaruma Dams
Nairobi
Narok
Mara River
Lake Victoria
Magadi
Athi River
Coast
Lamu
Garsen
Pate Island
Serengeti Plain
Kilimanjaro
Malindi
Voi
road to Kampalla
Tanzania
Mombasa
Masai Steppe
Indian Ocean
Pemba Island

KENYA

Chapter 2
Safari Encounters

IN KENYA, WE SETTLED IN THE HEART OF KIKUYU TRIBAL LANDS. OUR HOME WAS SURROUNDED BY COFFEE BUSHES ON ONE SIDE AND TEA BUSHES ON THE OTHER.

Five miles away, the deep gash of the Great Rift Valley soared downwards, and I was later to spend long tracts of my time roaming around the flatlands of the rift.

Each year, just before the rains were due, the Maasai set fire to the Ngong hills on the edge of the rift. No one knew how they could tell that the rains were coming, but as soon as the hills were seen enveloped in smoke, everybody knew the rains would start.

After the burn, all that was left was scorched soil and sooty rocks. Everything was burnt back, but with the rains the grass would return, thick and lush, and the Maasai would bring their cattle to graze. It was part of the ancient rhythm of their life.

On the far side of the hills there was an escarpment that was full of game. Lions, giraffes, zebras, Tommy gazelles, dik-diks, hyenas, tick birds, and nesting swallows all lived in profusion.

The escarpment was not part of the Nairobi Game Park—that tame tourist attraction was just outside the city. Nairobi was called the city where you could hear the roar of a lion. Maybe it had been one day, but that day was long gone. Now you could drive up the road toward the Ngong hills and turn left for the Wilson Airdrome or turn right into the game park. It was like going to the zoo. Very civilized.

Local Lore

The Kikuyu tribe is the largest in Kenya. Heavily agricultural, the girls are raised to tend to the farm and the boys are raised to tend to the cattle, sheep and goats. Kikuyu have a reputation for being hard-working and good with money, and while most of them still live on small farm plots, they have a desire for knowledge and believe that all children should receive a full education.

The escarpment was not like that. It was wild, well away from roads and well away from people. To go there was to enter a dangerous world where you were the weakest to walk the surface—unless you had a gun, and in those days, guns were not allowed. The Mau Mau wanted guns. To walk around with a gun was to invite trouble. The week that we arrived in Kenya two schoolboys had been murdered for their air rifle.

What kept you alive in the escarpment was knowledge. You had to know that a lion on a rock surrounded by females was good. A male lion alone on a rock was bad—the females were hunting. Never walk behind a giraffe; their rear feet would rip you from tip to toe. The most dangerous animal by far was the hyena. The hyena is clever, ruthless, and powerful; even the lion is afraid of the hyena and its crazy laughter. Snakes liked shadowy rocks and scorpions liked sandy crevices. Rhinos could not see, but they could hear and smell and they were bad tempered.

The Maasai would walk in the escarpment and be a part of it. Their ochre blankets and colored beads were as much a part of the scenery as the gray hide of a rhino. The blankets, under which they wore nothing, would flap around in the breeze. In Nairobi, tourists would ask to take pictures and then wait for a gust of wind. The moran, or warriors, would stand there, proudly arrogant in the pose and smiling at the stupidity of these white people who wanted a picture of their private parts.

The escarpment was too far away from my home to be my backyard. To go there took planning, but to me its flat-topped thorn trees, its endless vista stretching away to the Magadi salt flats, its dry heat, and its remoteness were the real Africa. I would go there with friends during the school holidays to play in the bush. It would always scare us with its simple wildness. It would have terrified my parents if they had known we were out there, but they never asked.

When I was ten, my grandparents came over to visit from England to see the real Africa. We drove up to the Queen Elizabeth National Park in Uganda. It was a wild place, like the escarpment.

Here I am by the Mara River while on safari.

On the way to the lodge, we came across a herd of elephants and stopped to watch them cross the road. My grandfather opened the car door, got out, and walked towards them. A large cow separated and challenged him, her head lowered, her ears raised in warning.

My mother in the front seat was yelling at my grandfather to get back in the car. My grandmother fainted. My father got out of the car to bring him back. When my father got out of the car, my mother's voice went up ten octaves and took on a hysterical note. My sister started to cry and I watched Dad as he slowly talked my Granddad away from the matriarch.

Granddad must have realized that his attempt to get a photograph standing alongside the herd had been an error in judgment.

He was now trying to extricate himself by waving his apology to the cow and backing away. The friendly apology by Granddad was misunderstood by the cow who raised her trunk and screamed. Anyone who has lived in Africa will tell you that this is the last warning before an elephant charges. My father knew it, I knew it, and my grandfather hadn't a clue.

My mother did, however, and she clamped her hand over the horn. The sound drew the cow's attention away from Granddad and to the car. The cow started to charge just as my grandmother was coming around from her faint. She yelped and fainted away again. My mom slid across into the driver's seat, slammed the car into reverse, and backed down the road.

When the cow saw the car backing away, she stopped charging and looked for the other distraction, but my father had pulled my granddad away from center stage and all was well. The cow went back to the herd she had protected, and my grandfather went back to the wrath of his wife and daughter.

After that we took great care to watch out for Granddad, who looked upon Africa as a large zoo. The safari took us into the Congo. We crossed Lake Albert in dugout wooden canoes, my grandfather singing the Eton boating song. The lake was full of hippos who look friendly but are not. They like to come up beneath canoes and tip them over. I knew it, my father knew it, and my grandfather didn't have a clue.

To go on safari in those early days was a true adventure. The road safari we took with my grandparents was one way of seeing the country. We drove from lodge to lodge and took side trips to see the animals. The other type of safari was the tented trip,

Local Lore

The hippo is considered to be one of the most dangerous animals in Africa. They kill more people every year than all the other African animals put together. In addition to the threat of having them tip over a canoe, hippos come ashore at night and anyone who has the misfortune to get between them and the water is likely to be attacked. With a land speed approaching 30 miles an hour and 20" incisors, these "aquatic teddy bears" are anything but cute.

where you set up a camp and lived there for weeks. We did that, too.

Percy Byers was our safari guide. He worked for the railroad—to be more specific, the East African Railways and harbors. He had a collection of rifles that gleamed. Their shiny wooden stocks and glistening oily barrels appeared ominous in the gloom of his study. He was a true white hunter—not the type who took the tourists out and wore a dinner jacket for dinner, but a real hunter. Percy had to go out with the railway crews to survey the lines and repair the tracks. He shot game for food and to protect the workers. He never shot for fun.

Percy shot game for food and to protect the workers. He never shot for fun.

Percy was stocky and bandy-legged. He wore a big, floppy hat with a strip of zebra skin around the crown. His eyes would crinkle as he spoke. His wife, a small woman in flowered dresses who knitted, traveled with him. She would sit in a canvas foldout safari chair and knit endless reams of woolen stuff. I never saw a complete garment.

The Mara River was wild, wilder than the escarpment. It was deep bush and you depended upon your own resources in the Mara. To get there you left Nairobi on the Nakuru road, and anywhere between mile forty-five and mile ninety you turned left off the road and headed southwest until you hit the river. When you reached the river you made camp because you had arrived.

The first order of business was to chop down a tree and lay it against another tree and a funk ladder. This gave you somewhere to run if you were attacked by something large. After that you would set the perimeter, set up the tents, set up the kitchen tents and the boys' quarters, and then go and find the game.

It was not difficult. They were right outside the perimeter. Within the space of an hour the trees around the tent would be alive with baboons and monkeys, chattering their news. The gossip was heard by the hyenas, and they would soon be seen with their distinctive sloped shoulders skulking among the trees. Then the birds would arrive, looking for leavings, and soon the camp would become a cacophony of sound—chirping, chattering, gibbering animals, all watching every move you made.

The baboons were the worst. The females would sport backsides of violent red. Their bottoms looked painful. They strutted on all fours with their arses jutting up in the air, splashes of truly impressive color paraded before the world. They had three-inch fangs and large snouts and small, piggy eyes. Baboons were not to be

Olive baboons. It's not their teeth that make them dangerous—it's their intelligence.

messed with. No one had to tell you this. One look at their teeth (or tushes) would tell you this was an angry animal to be avoided.

We had to move camp once because I threw a stone at a baboon. I had gone down to the river to fetch water. On the way down to the Mara, I came across a couple of baboons sitting under a tree. They were too near the path for my comfort, so I made them move by throwing a stone in their direction. They looked offended but got up and loped away.

I walked down to the river, being careful to avoid the crock slides. These were greasy mud slicks that a crocodile made with its tail where the bank fell steeply to the water's edge. The crocodile would then clamber on its short, stubby legs up to the top of the slide and wait for a small buck or a person to walk to the river.

Then, in one convulsive surge, it would slide down the bank, whipping its tail around the unsuspecting victim to tumble them into the water to be drowned. The carcass would be stuffed under the riverbank until the flesh rotted. The croc then returned to nibble on the tenderized, bloated body at its leisure. It was a fate to be avoided.

Finding a flat rock away from the crock slides, I filled up the canvas buckets and started back. As I rounded the bend, the two baboons I had pelted with a rock met me. They had come back with about thirty of their friends. I dropped the buckets and picked up a rock. They all reached down and picked up rocks. I dropped my rock. They didn't drop theirs. I started to run; they started to follow. I started to run really hard, I didn't look back. I made it back to the camp, closely followed by the pack. I flew into my father's tent, out of breath and begging forgiveness.

It was not immediately clear why I was begging for forgiveness. It soon becomes so. Every time I appeared, the baboons would leap up and down and throw broken branches at me. They formed a perimeter guard that would alert the pack whenever anyone tried to go to the river. Then they would all leap from the trees and throw rocks at the water bearer. After two days of this we broke camp and moved five miles down river. I had learnt my lesson: Never throw rocks at a baboon.

Years later when I brought my youngest son Rory to Africa to be christened, we stayed at the Muthaiga Club in Nairobi. A baboon watched us every day. On day three, it came to the door of our bungalow and tried to steal my son. The kidnapping was thwarted by my eldest son Brad, who was seven at the time. I wondered if the baboon tribe had put the word out that I was back in town. Impossible, of course, but who knows—this is Africa.

Chapter 3
Burning Bushes

By the time the Mau Mau rebellion had subsided, down to a few jungle fighters left to their own devices deep in the forests of Mount Kenya, my father had decided to resign from the army and take up civilian life.

We remained in our home surrounded by the coffee and tea bushes. I entered the lost years of teenage-hood, when banishment to my room became the most common form of parental discipline. This punishment taught me the joy and the endless pleasure of reading alone. By age fourteen I had finished War and Peace and had found Tolstoy's notes by far the most interesting part of the book. I read Seven Pillars of Wisdom by T.E. Lawrence and formed an opinion of the man that no movie or subsequent book has ever changed. I also read all of Winston Churchill's volumes on the Second World War, Eisenhower's Crusade in Europe, Douglas Bader's Reach for the Sky, Paul Brickwell's Escape from Colditz, and every other escape story I could find. I devoured books. I loved novels by Georgette Heyer, and other mid-seventeenth and eighteenth-century romances.

Reading was a passion—an open door that took me to other worlds. I experienced burning deserts with Lawrence or Napoleon's battlefields with Tolstoy. I soared with fighter pilots in the battle of Britain and quivered through depth charge attacks on British submarines. I suffered on the road to Mandalay and I fought at

Singapore. I was never bound by the fence posts of our Kiambu home. I was a reader. I was a time traveler.

True punishment was to be given a task.

"I want you to clear the hill behind the boys' quarters of Lantana, Barry." My father's voice was firm.

"Clear the hill? You mean the whole hill?"

"Yes, the whole hill."

"But that will take forever!"

"I know." There was a streak of cruelty in my father.

I faced the hill, a reluctant Jerroggee at my side. Jerroggee was my playmate and my partner in all things. He was fifty years old, with the heart of a child and the wisdom of a teenager. His role in the household was general helper, but mainly he used to hang out with me when I was around. He had no front teeth. He explained to me that they had been knocked out by his mother so she could feed him if he ever got lockjaw. The lack of teeth sometimes made him difficult to understand, but his grin was infectious and even my father would smile when Jerroggee would recount an exploit.

He explained to me that his teeth had been knocked out by his mother so she could feed him if he ever got lockjaw.

We faced the hill together. Lantana was vicious—a tough, flexible bush that had to be hacked to death. The wands of its branches were too thin to withstand the blow of a panga, the curved African blade that we used to cut wood and clear brush. The branches would slide away and then whip back at you. Curved thorns covered the branches. They would slice into the skin, leaving a thin trail of blood.

The broadleaf lantana shed its foliage constantly, so the bushes grew in a carpet of thick, dried leaves. This was home to snakes, rats, and hump-kneed spiders that would scurry over your shoes as you disturbed their habitat.

Lantana would grow to six to eight feet in height, so you worked in a constant gloom. As you worked, a fine cloud of moldy spores would rise up from the leaves and a shower of insects would fall on

Local Lore

The Maasai are a semi-nomadic people living in Kenya and Tanzania. Numbering some 500,000 people, they are one of the better known African indigenous tribes.

The Maasai believe that all of the cattle on the planet are a gift to them from God (Enkai), and their frequent cattle raids on neighboring villages aren't to steal cattle, but merely take back what is already theirs.

A Masaai traditionally could not take a wife until after he had killed a lion, a ceremony which was done in groups using spears and shields. The boy who speared the lion first was revered, and afforded special privileges throughout his life. This is one of many ceremonies which is little practiced now due to changes in the political and physical landscape.

your head from the branches above.

It was garden hell.

I was prepared. On my head I wore a soft, broad-brimmed safari hat, to stop the insects from falling down the back of my neck. I donned a long-sleeved, buttoned shirt and long safari trousers tucked into my boots. I topped all this off with a pair of leather gloves, and sunglasses in case the wands sprang back into my eyes.

Jerroggee wore his normal ganza, a length of cloth tied up between his legs. He was shoeless and hatless, but he was ready. Together we entered the lantana, sharpened pangas at our sides.

Hacking and slashing, we worked our way into the hill. The only way to effectively cut lantana was to grasp a branch, bend down to cut it at the base, pull it free, and throw it to the ground. After half an hour I was dripping with sweat, my arms were sore, my hat was covered with crawling insects, and my shirt sleeves were snagged in a hundred places.

Jerroggee was battered as well. His legs bore testament to the thorns. We stopped. We had cleared about twenty feet square. The hill loomed before us, at least five hundred yards wide and forty yards deep. It looked awe-inspiring.

"Let's take a break, Jerroggee," I said. I could tell that this was the best suggestion he had heard all morning. We sat on a log and looked up at the hill.

"The Maasai are burning the Ngong," Jerrogee said. I looked over toward the Ngong and saw the telltale spirals of smoke.

"The rains are coming," I said. Jerroggee nodded, his lips pursed in thought. At that moment a large snake slithered around the fresh cut stumps of the lantana and disappeared up the hill into the thick leaf cover. Jerroggee pursed his lips even more and drew his breath in sharply.

We continued to sit on the log.

"Perhaps we can learn from the Maasai, Bwana Barry," he said. I looked at him. He nodded toward the hill. "We can use fire to clear the old leafs. Then it will be easier to cut."

I looked sideways at Jerroggee. Then I looked up at the acres of lantana. I thought of the snake we had just seen disappear into the undergrowth. "Good idea," I said. "I know where there is a can of petrol."

"We will just make it a small fire, Bwana Barry. Just something we can burn away the taka taka."

It was the work of moments to get the petrol, pour a thin stream across the roots of three lantana bushes, and strike a match. It worked! Soon a nice little skirmish line of fire was working its way up the hill. The thick undergrowth developed a satisfying reddish glow as it simmered. The leaves of the lantana curled back in pain as the fire reached out and singed them. The whippy branches began to blacken. I felt an emotional satisfaction that I was causing this vicious plant agony. "So there!" I thought.

Jerrogee and I carefully advanced through the smoking undergrowth and began hacking at the blackened wands. From nowhere, the lightest zephyr of a breeze appeared—just a kiss upon the cheek. I looked up. The little skirmish line had felt it as well. The tendrils of fire wavered, then leapt up to six feet in height. Crackling sounds were heard as the top branches of the wands met the flames. Blackened leaves began to waltz into the sky.

"Aaaaahhhhhh," I heard Jerroggee say. It was a sound that was familiar to me. It was not good.

Maasai Moran warriors. The spears are traditionally used for hunting lions.

"Get the water hose, Jerroggee." I needn't have bothered. Jerroggee was already galloping across the lawn in the direction of the garden boy. He soon reappeared with the hose and the garden boy, who stood there grinning.

"Maji" (water) I yelled. I had to yell as the crackle had developed into a roaring sound. I looked back at the fire. The skirmish line was no more. In its place was a wall of flame, flickering and consuming all in its path. Birds were shooting into the air, and a plume of dark smoke covered the hillside. I began to cough in the smoke. The heat was intense.

"Ahhhhhhhhhhhhhhhhhhh!" Jerroggee was in fine form today. The garden boy started to snicker.

"Bwana Barry." I looked at Jerroggee standing with the hose, spluttering a completely inadequate supply of water for our needs. "Bwana Barry, Bwana McCloud."

I jumped in my skin. Our next-door neighbors' house was on the other side of the hill. It was a good half-mile away, but the way the flames were surging up the hill it would not be long before they would reach the crest. On the other side of the crest was a series of vegetable gardens, the main house, the servants' quarters, and then row upon row of tea seedling bushes—all waiting in the path of the roaring inferno I had created. Actually, it had been Jerroggee's suggestion, but legal parsing was not going to save me if I burnt down John's place.

John McCloud had a tea nursery. Traditionally, tea propagates via seeds. When the seed germinates—i.e., cracks its shell and lets a root wiggle out—it will take a year before the slender plant has a chance of survival. The roots love rich, acid-type soil, and do not flourish in dry environments. The seed develops a taproot that seeks water and can grow up to five feet long—longer if it is exposed on a bank.

Within five years, the slender bush has developed enough leaves to begin contributing to the overall yield of the estate. Every seven years, the bush is pruned so that its top, or table, remains flat and easy to pluck. It is the fresh, young buds that are picked, and they are always, or almost always, surrounded by two little leaves—hence the expression, "two leaves and a bud."

Nowadays, no one expands by using seeds. Today, tea bushes are cloned by taking cuttings from high-yielding bushes and then growing hundreds of such cuttings so that the tea fields can be calculated to produce fairly precise amounts of tea. This was John's setup. He had rows of cutting sleeves, then beyond them yearly cuttings in beds, and beyond them the plants ready for sale. A roaring inferno would devastate the garden, but at that point it would have already consumed the house and I would be a dead man.

"I'll tell him," I yelled and ran down the driveway and then over to McCloud's home. I remember flying over the ground, but I arrived at his front door exhausted. I pounded on the door, no sense of decorum left. When Mr. McCloud opened the door, all I could do was point at the forest fire that was now running the entire length of the ridge.

"Jesus Christ" was all John said before disappearing back into his house. He gathered his house servants to fight the fire. I sat on the doorstep, my world in tatters. There was no way of hiding a blackened hillside from my father. I thought about running away to sea. Did they still hire cabin boys?

Tea Tales

When you visit an old tea estate, you see many different colored bushes, all with different leaf shapes, this being a sure sign that the bushes came from seeds. When you visit a newly planted tea field, there is a common color and leaf shape for acre upon acre. In the early morning sun or the last rays of the day it can be a breathtaking sight. However, cloned teas, like purebred dogs, fall prey to all sorts of diseases and pests. In order to protect the fields from being eaten by a bug to which it has no resistance, new estates have fields of different clones to avoid catastrophic losses should some voracious bug appear.

Tea-producing countries, such as India and Ceylon, have large tea research centers where the needs of their particular country are met and problems are solved. They develop different types of fertilizer applications, how to reduce pest activity, and maximize yields from tea bushes that are nearing the end of their growth cycle.

John McCloud had cleared his land of lantana many years prior. The fire had nothing to feed on and slowly died away. It managed to consume about an acre of his maize field before slowly ending its life by the irrigation ditch.

As John walked back toward his house, I saw my father's car pull into the driveway. It crunched its way up to us. My father got out and looked at the blackened hillside, the burnt maize field, then at John, and finally at me.

"I saw the smoke, John. Thought I would come back and see what my son was up to. Sorry about the maize. May I settle up with you later?"

"Of course, Roland. Gave us quite a scare. Glad Barry warned me in time."

My father looked at me. "Kind of him," he said, in his driest tone.

I thought of various explanations, but none came to mind apart from the truth. "The Maasai burn the hills. I thought it might work here."

"The Maasai burn unpopulated, remote grazing areas, where the grass is less than two feet high, Barry. They do not burn lantana. No one burns lantana. If you try and burn lantana, it tends to catch fire. It spreads. Only an idiot would try and clear lantana by burning it. Where's Jerroggee?"

But Jerroggee was nowhere to be found. He had a knack of disappearing. It was one thing he never taught me. I was confined to barracks again. I don't think my father knew what else to do with me. I was forbidden to touch anything or do anything. I was just to be.

Chapter 4

Seventeen and Searching

THOUGH I LEFT HIGH SCHOOL WITH SURPRISINGLY GOOD GRADES, I WISHED TO START MY LIFE AND NOT CONTINUE THE SLOG OF ENFORCED EDUCATION.

I had a clash of wills with my parents and I won—mainly because my parents were so involved in fighting each other, they had no time to include me in the battles. They gave up and I was free to enter the workforce. I wanted to write.

Through my father's contacts, I was given an opportunity to join Nairobi's local newspaper, the *Daily Nation* as a junior sports reporter. I had my own column in the Sunday edition—writing about the comings and goings of teenagers in and around Nairobi.

In those days, the city was the center for all the overseas correspondents covering central Africa for all the English newspapers and magazines. They were a group of hard-drinking, hard-living, worldly wise men, and here was I, a seventeen-year-old mascot.

It was 1962 and the Belgian Congo was going up in flames. The Simba, a group of drug-crazed rebels, were shooting and raping their way across Kinshasa. Dag Hammarskjöld, the UN secretary general, was shot out of the sky over the Congo. Refugees were flooding into Uganda and Kenya.

The correspondents were in the midst of a period of turmoil, danger, global politics, confusion, and great stories, and I was in the midst of the correspondents. It shakes me now to think of the risks I ran in those days, but fueled by Martel brandy, the bravado of being one of the guys, and the rough-and-ready camaraderie that is part of being an elite group, I lived a life way beyond my years.

At this point, my parents had given up the ghost of their marriage and I was living with my father. He saw where my life was heading and took me aside, gave me a round-trip ticket to England, and told me not to use the return half.

I was on my way. My hard-drinking friends gave me a farewell party and a letter of introduction to the *Newcastle Evening Chronicle*. It had come my turn to go, though I didn't have a clue what was waiting for me. I was only seventeen.

England was a shock to my ego and my system. I was cold and I was anonymous, one of millions. I took jobs as a construction worker, a demolition worker, and a garage mechanic as I waited for the golden invitation to arrive from Newcastle. When it did arrive, I took the next train up to that grim city.

LOCAL LORE

In the early '60s a group of Congolese rebeled against their government. Being animastic people, the Congolese were told by their witch doctors they were immune to bullets and would turn into *Simbas* (the Swahili word for lions) when entering battle. In a sense the magic worked—40 rebels and their witch doctors stormed the city of Stanleyville and routed a military force of over 1,500 men who were armed with mortars and armored vehicles. The Simba never fired a single shot. Numerous other fights had similar outcomes, with hundreds of well-armed militia fleeing before the Simba in terror. The rebellion only lasted a period of a year or so, but during that time the Simbas killed around 10,000 civilians. I'm not sure how that was much of an improvement over the previous government.

Newcastle nestles against the North Sea. It is opposite Norway, and it is cold and wet most of the time. Its first major industry was coal mining; it made a lot of sense to me that they would want to spend as much time as possible underground.

The editor read my cuttings and offered me a position. The newspaper had a scholarship program—I would work at the newspaper and go to the local university. The world lay before me. I lived in Whitley Bay, a seaside resort that was stark and gray. My landlady was Mrs. Leach, a large-bosomed lady who cooked very greasy eggs for breakfast.

The horrible reality of Newcastle slowly settled upon me. I could not understand the local people when they spoke; the thick Geordie accent was beyond me. This was a major disadvantage for a reporter. After the fourth or fifth "excuse me, can you repeat that," the interview trails away. It was a problem I could never overcome.

The horrible reality of Newcastle slowly settled upon me.

I was doomed from the start. A work routine that took away every weekend, so that when I had a day off, everybody else was at work, did not help. The city was old, broken-down, its industries of coal and shipbuilding a thing of the past. About half the population were unemployed, and I could not understand the people. I decided to make a clean break. I was not destined to be a reporter, certainly not in Newcastle.

I moved to London. I arrived penniless. Years of tradition pulled me to the security of the armed forces. I enlisted in the Royal Marines. A full day of examinations—medical, physical, and mental—ended with the surprise news that they would contact me in a month. They could not take me now.

So I got a job in a "breakers yard" breaking up cars. They gave me an oxyacetylene torch and led me to a wrecked car at the back of the yard. The foreman, Fred, showed me how to work the torch and then told me to cut the car up.

A therapist could not have chosen a more healing task. I set to work and I contentedly reduced the car to bits and pieces. They called me "his lordship" because my accent was different. There was Fred the foreman and Mr. Blackman the crane operator, an old hunched man with a spotted scalp and very little hair. His son, Joe, drove the pickup truck to collect all the wrecks, and the owner of the yard, Mr. Smith, wore an elegant topcoat.

As the Marines processed my application I thought about where life was taking me. My military ancestry included relatives

Getty Images

The breakers yard was very cathartic, as I spent the day hacking up cars.

who had signed up under the same circumstances and made the military their home. Did I want to fight foreign wars, in far off lands? My father, his two brothers, my grandfather, my great-grandfather, my great-great-grandfather had all joined the colors.

I decided to choose a different path. I chose not to go. When the sign-up papers arrived, I sent them back. Wherever my life was to lead me it was not to be down the throat of an enemy musket, or so I thought.

I remained in the breakers yard for two years. My muscles became hard again. Eventually, I bought real workman shirts of blue denim and jeans and work boots. My hands became callused. I learnt to strip an engine of any part for resale. Pistons, carburetors, driveshafts, rear axles—you name it, I could remove it.

The crashes that came in were spectacular, and the yard must have been full of ghosts at night. I have no way of knowing how long I would have stayed there. One morning I woke in drastic pain. The doctor made a house call; he diagnosed gastroenteritis. The pain would not go away, and the only comfort was soaking in a bath of warm water. I began to vomit up green bile, twenty-four hours later the doctor said I might have appendicitis and sent me to the hospital in an ambulance. After twelve hours and a lot of tests, they found I had a stone lodged in my urethra. They told me that they were very surprised to find a twenty-year-old with a stone in his kidney, but after forty-eight hours of pain I was so grateful for a diagnosis that I didn't care. The pain was so bad I had taken to clutching a Bible. They operated on me and pushed the stone back into my kidney. I spent a week waiting to see if it passed. It didn't, so they cut it out.

During the week I was waiting to pass the stone, I served tea to the other patients in the ward. I saw men come in; I would give them tea. The next day the bed would be empty, stripped of its mattress. The patient had died in the night. It always came as a shock.

After the operation, I was in hospital for a week recovering. They sent me home with a scar that runs from my backbone to my groin and instructions to not do any heavy lifting for six months. My career in the breakers yard was over and I began to cast about for other options.

Angus, my sister's boyfriend and son of the manager of the Mau Forest tea estate in Kenya, was working for Lipton as a trainee tea taster. He was posted to Calcutta. A position was open, and Angus suggested I write to Lipton. I did, and after a series of interviews, I was asked back for a final meeting.

The tea director at Lipton, a man named Wilmshurst, sat on the right hand of God. Tall and imposing, with an eye that could freeze a head waiter or a poor trainee at fifty paces, he was not one to trifle with. Our final meeting went well. Not a word was spoken of tea. We discussed cricket and the wisdom of playing a man at short leg (not a good idea we both agreed, unless the bowler was deadly accurate). I felt I made points with that. We both loved rugby, so I felt things were going well. When he stood up I was sure the interview was over. Instead, he asked me if I knew the chairman.

"No." I had never met the man.

"Well, he appears to know you," was the response. "And he would like to see you."

Stunned, I followed Wilmshurst down a long corridor into a huge office with a huge desk, behind which sat a smiling Buddha of a man.

"Here's Cooper," said Wilmshurst and left.

"Sit down my boy, sit down," said the Buddha. "Now tell me, I see that you have given Gilbert Lee as a reference. Do you know Gilbert well?"

"He's my uncle, sir," I replied. He was also chairman of all the British Airways associated companies, hotel chains, food companies, and assorted airlines around the world. I thought he would be a good person to put down as a reference.

"Ahhh," said the Buddha. "So Kathleen is your aunt?"

In a flash of light I saw where this was going. "Yes, sir; actually, Kathleen is my father's sister. She really is my aunt."

"Ahhh. How is she, my boy?"

"She is as stunning as ever, sir," which was true. My aunt had movie star good looks, long slender legs, and even at fifty was a knockout.

"Ahhhhhhhhhh," was the only response for a moment. A long pause followed. "I squired your aunt to many functions when I was a younger man, back in the '30s," the Buddha said with a whimsical smile. "Do give her my best when you next speak to her."

I was in. My career in tea had begun.

Chapter 5 Lipton Training

I had come home. At the first sight of a tearoom, with its white porcelain china, I knew this was what I wanted to do.

Tasting tea came easy for me. The millions of little facts and details that you had to learn were salve to my soul. I absorbed tea. I loved its heritage, the stories, the smells, and the tastes. I loved the tradition and the feel of the different teas. It has never changed. To this day, I am happiest tasting and blending tea.

The tea buying and blending center for Lipton was at Allied Suppliers, an aged building in the heart of London Cockney land. A single elevator that could hold two people ran up to the top floor. From there, you had to walk through the warehouse, past the men opening tea chests with claw hammers, pulling out the nails that fastened the metal bands to the plywood one by one. Then you went on past the blend lines, where the tea chests, originating from around the world, were lined up in blend sequence to be toppled into the huge blending drum. The drum groaned as it slowly revolved, tipping the tea endlessly until it was completely blended. Then finally, at the far end of the building where the northern light poured in through huge skylights, you entered the hallowed halls of the tasting room.

I was told that tasters always needed northern light, as it was constant and we would not suffer from bright sun or fading shadows that might influence our judgment. Such an understanding ensured that tea tasters got the best view a building had to offer.

Tea Tales

There is no difference between white, black, green, and oolong tea. All tea comes from the same species of tea plant, called *Camellia sinensis*. It is the process that makes a tea different, not the tea bush itself. Once the leaves are picked, they are allowed to oxidise for different periods of time. This produces different colors in the leaves, and also different flavors when steeped. White teas are oxidised the least, followed by green, oolong, and black. Black tea is the most popular tea in western countries, and usually has an oxidation period anywhere from two weeks to a month.

Herbal tea doesn't contain tea at all—it is simply an infusion made from different fruits, berries or herbs.

The tasting room was divided into four counters, long benches on which the tea was prepared. To the right as you entered was the blending counter, ruled over by Mr. Alford, a huge man with a mighty girth and a friendly manner. He prepared all the blends for the Lipton range of products.

Next came the Ceylon counter, which brewed up only Ceylon teas, and on the far left was the Assam, India, and others, which brewed up everything else from Vietnams, to Turkish, and all the way through to the finest Darjeelings and Assams.

The entire tasting room was surrounded by hundreds upon hundreds of shelves filled with heavily lidded tin boxes holding last week's auction purchases. The room was a hive of quiet industry: a steady hum of kettles spouting steam, lids clattering as teas were brewed, master tasters and their apprentices slurping and spitting, and all permeated with the wonderful smell of freshly brewed tea. It was heaven!

I started out on the Ceylon counter. A young Ceylonese taught me how to weigh and brew the teas. Within a week, I was competent and fast at preparing the hundreds of cups that we had to taste each day.

Getty Images

A typical tea tasting.

We would heat up large copper kettles with long, curved spouts on a gas stove. As the water was heating, we would measure two pennyweight (five grams) into a handheld balance and tip the loose tea into a white porcelain mug with serrated edges. We would go down the counter, which held six trays holding eight mugs and bowls each, for a total of forty-eight sets. When the water boiled, we would run down and pour an inch of boiling water into the bottom of each mug so that each mug started to brew at the same time.

Then we would return and top off the mugs and place the lids on. When we had gone the length of the counter, we would set the timer for six minutes. When the timer sounded, we would tip the mug into the bowl so that it was at an angle and the tea poured into the bowl and the leaves would be trapped against the serrated edges. Then we would go back and tip the tea leaves into the lid of the mug and place the mug bending the bowl of tea. The master taster would then be able to see the dry leaf, the infused leaf, and the brewed tea all at one glance.

We would do this ten times a day, three days a week. We would taste every single tea, and as trainees we were supposed to taste more than just once. That is about three thousand cups of tea a week. You get used to it, or you leave to become a merchant banker as a couple of the trainees did. It was just too much for them.

After being taught how to prepare tea, a trainee was then taught how to slurp tea from a spoon into his mouth, deep into the caverns of his tonsils, and then to swirl it around, breathing in at the same time. One had to avoid the cardinal sin of choking and spraying his tea master with a fine mist. It was an art, and it took weeks of practice and choking to finally develop my own "slurp." Every taster has his own distinctive slurp, and after a few weeks I could tell which tea master was in the room without looking up.

The head tea buyer—an august, small man by the name of E.A. Locke, or "Lockie" to everybody except us lowly trainees—had a gentle sip, almost ladylike. Mr. Rossi, on the other hand, had a gargantuan slurp like a man truly enjoying soup with no one within earshot.

After preparing the counter I would stand by the master taster, Mr. Mackie, as he would go down the bench. Four stars, two stars, burnt no good (NG). I would mark the catalog and make note of the companies that would be interested in each of the various teas. There would be great excitement when an order would come in from Japan or America, as this meant that the best quality teas were to be bid on. He would tell me what teas were good and why they were good. He would smell the dry leaf and the wet leaf, and taste the brewed tea—all in the space of thirty seconds. He'd make a comment, then move on to the next one. I was supposed to note the comment, write it down, taste the tea, then move to the next tea.

In my tasting room in Boulder, Colorado, I have the exact same setup—same bowls, same lids, same mugs, same scales. I have been to tasting rooms all over the world; they all have the same equipment. It is identical. We can compare notes with other professionals a continent away, because we know we prepare the tea the same way. Tradition is a wonderful thing.

Each tea had a code name. Gull, Quail, and Eagle all meant a certain grade and quality. Each Friday the cables would be sent out to the buying companies: 500 Gull available at 610, meaning

500 chests of tea of Gull quality at a price of six shillings and ten pence.

On Monday, the orders would be waiting for us and the trainees and the buyer would leave for the London auction to bid on the teas. The auction would be held at Plantation House on Mincing Lane, the home of the tea trade. The auction room was a two-storied amphitheatre, surrounded by the crests of foreign lands from whence came the tea. The auctioneer would sit in the pit, with a jobbing broker on either side of him to take bids from the smaller buyers. We would sit behind our buying brokers and lean forward to whisper our bids. This practice was supposed to keep secrecy intact. The trainee would keep a record of all the prices for each lot and the prices that the buyer paid for the lots we purchased.

I had to keep a running average of the prices (this was before the age of calculators). The lots were sold at about five a minute—it was fast. Panic would set in if you fell behind, because it was impossible to catch up. Mr. Mackie was a nervous buyer. He had been the managing director of Lipton Ceylon, but for some reason had been recalled and was now a simple buyer. He would twitch and roll his eyes as he bid on teas and would constantly ask for the average. His broad Scots accent would thicken as the other buyers bid him up.

It became clear to me after a few weeks of attending the auction as an assistant that the auction was a big game to the large buyers, such as Lyons, Brooke Bond, and Co-op. They had the resources to bid up on teas and stick some poor buyer with a lot that he could not afford. Breaks of tea would come in lots of sixty chests or more. If four buyers wanted some of the tea but each buyer wanted twenty chests, there was not enough to go round, so the buying bidder would say, "Twenty Lyons, twenty Brookes, forty Co-op; Lipton, you are out." This meant that Lipton had to bid up the price to see if one of the other buyers would drop out. If they all dropped out at the same time, Lipton got stuck with sixty chests of tea when they only wanted twenty. Everybody would snicker. It was all harmless, really. After the auction, private deals would be made and the forty unwanted chests would easily find a home.

At the end of the auction, Mackie would sigh with relief. What seemed to me as fun was to him an ordeal. The next day, we would receive the contracts. The trainees would have to go through them and check the contract against the catalog to make sure the price and the lot were correct. That afternoon, a half-pound sample of the tea we had purchased would come in (the purchase sample). We would taste it against the offer sample and then box the purchase sample. When they were all tasted and approved, we would make a bulk-up of the teas and send out a small sample of Gull or Quail to the buying company. At the same time, we were tasting next week's teas. On Friday, the cables would go out and the whole process would start again.

London was the best place to train for a career in tea in the early '60s. The London auction was a powerful center. Teas from all over the world would be sent there for sale. In one place, you could taste Assam, Darjeelings, Vietnams, Indonesians, Ceylons, Japanese oolongs, South Indians, even Turkish teas.

I lived in the northwest of London and took the underground every day. I became a commuter—one of the nameless many who swayed in the train as it made its way into the center of London. I learnt to time my arrival at the train station seconds before my train arrived. I learnt to change at Finchely Road onto an express if my timing was right. I was surrounded by gray and blue suits, morning newspapers, and umbrellas. I was part of the masses. It felt very strange. I would sit or stand and dream of Kenya, or some other far-off land where they grew tea and hope.

My destination was Liverpool Street Station, a looming, glass-paned survivor of Hitler's bombing. I would walk up Liverpool Street to the tea warehouse on Bethnal Green Road, in the East End of London, where all the Cockneys lived.

The Bethnal Green building and tasting room are no more, but if you turn to page 60 of Ukkers *All about Tea*, Vol II, first published in 1935, you will see the room I trained in. It is fixed in posterity forever. Sadly, the London auction is also no more. It ceased to exist as the countries that grow tea took control of their own destiny. I experienced the end of hundreds of years of tradition and history. I felt honored to have been a part of the old trading ways. I still do.

For two years, I worked at the benches in London, switching between the North Indian counter, the blending counter, and the Ceylon counter. I was constantly learning more as I went along. E.A. Locke, he of the ladylike sip, was a giant in the industry. Locke was a man of few words but a wicked sense of humor. He once came out to taste a batch of teas I had prepared and started immediately. The only problem was that the spittoon was at the far end of the bench. He started to give his comments on the teas, which of course I had to write down, thus not giving me enough time to dash down to the end of the counter to get the spittoon. Locke happily went down the entire back, spitting out the tea onto the wooden floor, a wide grin on his face. I never left the spittoon at the end of the counter again.

Locke happily went down the entire back, spitting out the tea onto the wooden floor, a wide grin on his face.

After two years, I felt I had gained all there was to learn at the counters and I wanted to go overseas; but no work visas were available. Newly independent countries were looking to hire and train their own tea men. I had to wait. I was offered a job by Lipton in their supermarket division, but I chose to resign and seek my own fortune. Besides, my mother was coming over from Kenya on a visit. It was the first time I had seen her in five years.

I greeted her at the airport with a single rose. She had not written in five years, nor had she offered to help me get back to Kenya for my sister's wedding two years earlier. The wounds were deep but papered over. We toured Ireland together and it was a time of reconnecting. Come back to Kenya my mother said, I'll pay for the ticket.

I left England with little regret. We flew on a charter airline that declared bankruptcy as we were in the air. We landed in Nairobi and my father hugged me. I was home. I was back in Africa.

Chapter 6
The Brothel

"I WOULD RATHER BE LUCKY THAN GOOD" HAS BEEN A MANTRA OF MINE FOR YEARS. SO MUCH OF MY LIFE HAS BEEN JUST PURE GOOD FORTUNE.

When I arrived back in Kenya, my sister and her husband had just moved into a new house. They mentioned to their landlord that I was returning to Kenya; the landlord and his company in Mombasa were looking for a tea taster! A few days later I was flying in a small, single-engine plane down to Mombasa. The pilot, Peter Winch, was owner of the tea and coffee company. Winch was a larger-than-life figure—rotund, bearded, and loud. A Kenya character.

"Lean forward as we take off," he yelled as we sped down the runway at Wilson Airdrome. "I think we are a touch heavy." He said this as the end of the runway rapidly approached. We cleared the fence surrounding the airdrome by a few feet. " Ahh...up at last," yelled Peter, clearly enjoying my discomfort.

We landed for lunch at Mtito Andei, the halfway point between Mombasa and Nairobi. Peter angled the plane down and swooped over a game lodge. "Who's hungry?" he yelled.

A couple appeared on the steps of the lodge, and Peter waggled the wings and then swept low over the dirt landing strip. "Just chasing off the warthogs. Last trip, damn near hit one. Would've ruined lunch."

We landed and a Land Rover appeared with the couple driving to haul us over to the lodge. I was back in Africa with a vengeance.

Tea Tales

Mombasa was, and still is, a major auction center. Teas from Kenya, Uganda, Rwanda, Burundi, the Congo, and Tanzania all made their way down to Mombasa to be auctioned.

The main tea-growing region in Kenya in the late 1950s and early '60s was in Kericho, a good day's drive from the capital, Nairobi. Most of the estates were owned by large corporations located in Great Britain, like Brooke Bond and Finlays. Around the early 1960s, the British government started the Kenya Tea Development Authority (KTDA), which was initially a small holder project. This meant that small farmers would grow an acre of tea, more or less. They would harvest every seven days and take the tea to a central processing plant where they would sell it. This scheme became one of the most successful tea projects ever and has propelled Kenya to become one of the largest tea exporters in the world. In 2002, they produced over 250,000 metric tons of tea and exported most of it. By expanding the tea fields in the '60s, the KTDA was able to make use of the most modern technology available at the time.

Mombasa was hot and steamy, and the approach over the putrid swamps was bumpy and eventful, with Peter yelling at me to open the door as we rolled down the runway. "Got to slow us down, old boy!"

The next day, I was picked up and taken to the offices in the industrial area to meet the tea team. The shortest job interview in the world is for a tea taster.

"Here are twelve teas. What are their origins, what are the grades, how much are they worth on today's market, who would use them?"

You either know what you are doing, or you don't. I did. I got the job.

After the gloom of London, Mombasa was a joy. I moved into The Castle Hotel, which offered me a three-month stay at reduced rates. Breakfast, lunch, and dinner were part of the deal. The Castle was a large, white hotel on Kenyatta Avenue. Scalloped windows sat beneath a turreted roof. It had pretensions of grandeur. It was also the local brothel of choice.

The girls hung out in the arched patio bar, which stretched from the foyer to the street. Sailors, Arabs, locals, visiting businessmen, and all manner of brothel clientele would pay courtesy stops. The girls made their deals and took their customers upstairs.

My room was on the second floor, facing the courtyard. After a while, I became a fixture and the girls lost interest in me as a potential client. My mother came to visit and stayed at the hotel. She was mistaken for one of the girls, and an Asian gentleman took a lot of convincing that she was not for rent. After my mother's visit I became part of the fraternity, included in their chatter and gossip.

I learnt about the foibles of mankind: the elderly gentleman who took so long he was prepared to pay double; the young man who was so quick he always tried to negotiate a discount; the seamen who wanted to double up, and sometimes triple up on a girl; the local business leaders who would slip in the back and call down to the front for their girlfriends. I met a few of them on the staircase.

> **The Castle was a large, white hotel on Kenyatta Avenue. Scalloped windows sat beneath a turreted roof. It had pretensions of grandeur. It was also the local brothel of choice.**

Nothing is stranger than two men meeting in the stairwell of a brothel. They both presumably know why they are there. This provides instant simpatico and comradeship. But the nature of the business requires a certain formality. There were those who slunk around, face averted, and those who strode up the center of the staircase. Often it depended on whether they were walking up the stairs or coming down. I gained a certain reputation until someone discovered I lived there. It caused amusement.

I learnt that the girls were all concerned with the mundane issues of life—enough money for food, for clothes, for their children, their boyfriends, and sometimes their parents. They

Local Lore

AIDS has had a devastating effect in Africa. In some areas infection rates are approaching 40%, and over 12,000,000 children have been left orphaned. A lot of this is due to a lack of education on the disease and limited access to health care and condoms. The effect it has had on economic productivity has been staggering, and this catch-22 means that the more people that become infected, the fewer resources are available to try and prevent the spread of the disease. Some progress has been made in recent years, but there's still a long way to go.

had cliques and friendships and were united only in their hatred of the police and customers who tried to cheat them. They had their favorites and their regulars. To sit with them and listen to their chatter was to be included in a rare group. It was like being surrounded by a flock of exotic birds.

They were young girls from a variety of tribes, yet they created their own tribe. Their tribe had its own customs. Woe betide a member who tried to steal a regular customer from another. Or offered herself at lower rates. Or stole. They had their own code, their own sense of honor. When the fleet was in town, they would band together against the hundreds of young women who would come down from up-country to service the sailors. Then there would be catfights and a simmering rivalry between the Mombasa regulars and the interlopers.

The Castle Hotel is still there, a sad sight now: boarded up, the brilliant white exterior gray and stained with the dripping of broken gutters. When I was last there I peered through boards at the cracked patio. It was covered in debris and weeds. I remembered the gaiety and the risky sense of fun. It was better that way. AIDS has devastated Africa now, and careless sex is no more. It would not be possible to even think of living the way I did then. I hope they all survived.

I was sad to leave after my three months were up, but I had been told that it was inappropriate to live in a brothel. I moved in with a young bank trainee in his bank-provided house. The house was in Nyali, an upmarket residential area and a very appropriate address. But I missed the girls and would go back and have a beer with them. They always welcomed me with high-pitched giggles. I was never treated as a potential customer but as a returning member of the tribe. I felt honored.

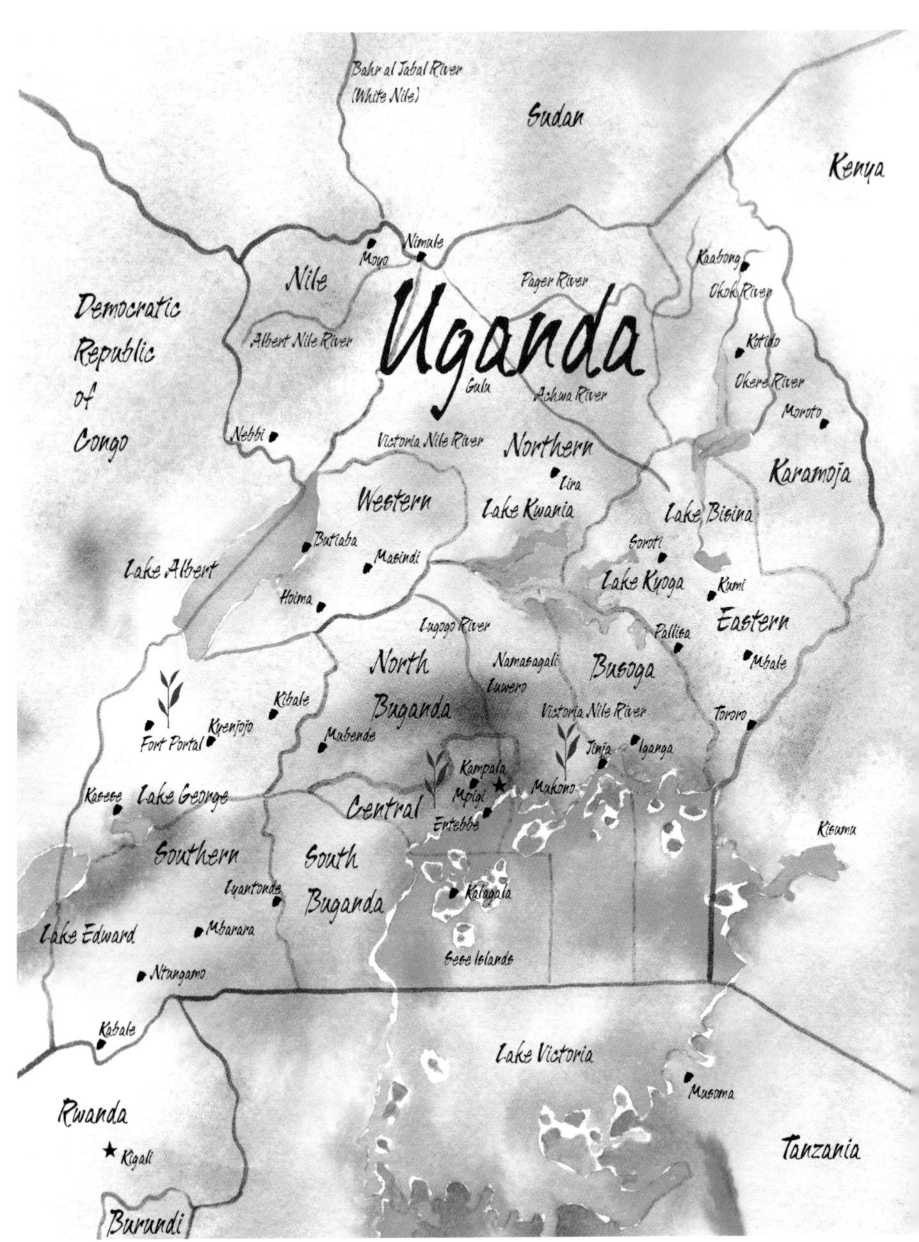

Bahr al Jabal River
(White Nile)
Sudan
Kenya
Nimule
Moyo
Nile
Kaabong
Pager River
Okok River
Democratic
Republic
of
Congo
Albert Nile River
Uganda
Kotido
Gulu
Achwa River
Okere River
Moroto
Nebbi
Victoria Nile River
Northern
Karamoja
Lira
Western
Lake Kwania
Lake Bisina
Butiaba
Soroti
Masindi
Lake Albert
Lake Kyoga
Kumi
Hoima
Eastern
Lugogo River
Pallisa
North
Namasagali
Busoga
Mbale
Luwero
Kibale
Buganda
Victoria Nile River
Tororo
Kyenjojo
Fort Portal
Mubende
Jinja
Iganga
Kampala
Kasese
Lake George
Mpigi
Mukono
Central
Entebbe
Kisumu
Southern
South
Lyantonde
Buganda
Kalagala
Lake Edward
Mbarara
Sese Islands
Ntungamo
Kabale
Lake Victoria
Musoma
Rwanda
Tanzania
Kigali
Burundi

UGANDA

Chapter 7
Uganda Bound

IN THE '50S AND '60S, KENYA WAS STILL YOUNG AND FULL OF ECCENTRIC CHARACTERS WHO MADE A POINT OF THEIR ECCENTRICITY.

Known as the dumping ground of the English gentry and their second and third sons—and occasionally a ne're-do-well first son—in the '20s and '30s it was still a land of adventurers, rascals, scoundrels, businessmen, soldiers, and white hunters. The white population of Kenya never amounted to more than one hundred thousand people, even at the height of the settler movement, but our time was doomed even as we lived it.

I entered a culture clash in the small Kenyan tasting room. The three of us who worked there, Don Lowe, Mick Clark, and I, were like oil and water. Don—precise, neat, and meticulous in every detail—was destined to perish in a terrible accident many years later when he was thrown from a car. Mick Clark was a quintessential trader, wheeling and dealing. Finally there was me, for whom details have always been an issue and playing rugby was more important, quite frankly, than staying late at work. For six months we tried to make it work. Then Peter came to me and asked me if I would like to move to Uganda and to open up the country and establish a trading office. I was twenty-three years old. I said, "Yes."

I left a week later. I had 400 sample bags, six tasting cups and lids, a tea scale, my tasting spoon, and an optimistic outlook.

I stopped in Nairobi to see my family; it was as dysfunctional as ever.

I stayed for a week in Nairobi then moved on. It was a three-day drive from Mombasa to Kampala, the capital of Uganda. The border was at Jinja, where Lake Victoria empties into the Nile River. The drive through the northern part of Kenya was dry and dusty. Endless vistas of gray scrub stretched before me under an arched blue sky. Cross the border and you were in a new world of greenery: lush vegetation, banana trees, soaring jungles, and miles of water-saturated papaya grass. The road runs like an arrow, straight through the heart of the papaya swamps. A narrow ridge of a dyke ends in a shimmering mirage during the day, and pitch-black darkness at night.

The sounds are different in Uganda. There are more birds, the air is wet and slightly musty, and the heat of Kenya gives way to a languid softness.

The sounds are different in Uganda. There are more birds, the air is wet and slightly musty, and the heat of Kenya gives way to a languid softness. It is a more violent country; gangs roam the land. A lone European is easy bait.

I arrived in Kampala at dusk. There was a brilliant sunset and then the sudden darkness of Africa. The city sits astride seven hills, and the roads curve in and around and up and down. I drove through the clatter which is the evening and made my way to the Apollo Hotel, high above the town.

George Kargarottas, a barrel-chested Greek, was there to meet me. He ran the coffee trading business for Peter Winch, and I was to run the tea. George was the one issuing my paycheck, so I took him to be the boss. He responded well to that approach, so I kept it up.

"Have a beer; tell me what you are supposed to be doing up here; I know nothing about tea—except it's grown in all the dangerous places around here."

"Dangerous, huh?" I said, trying to sound very nonchalant.

"Very!" said George, taking a deep draft of his beer and looking over the rim of his glass at me. "I think you should hit the road tomorrow and go up to the growing region, stay there for a couple of weeks."

"Tomorrow, huh?" I replied, trying the nonchalant approach again.

"You should learn the lay of the land and the growers, drive around, get yourself comfortable, learn the ropes—where to go, where not to go."

"Where not to go, huh?"

"You were raised in Kenya, right? Speak the language, right? Know Africa, right? Can handle yourself, right?"

"Ah...sure," was my only response as I buried my face inside my glass and sought some Dutch courage.

After about six large beers, I vaguely remember telling George that I was ready to leave that night—get-started-early type of thing—and George telling me that tomorrow would be fine. He also told me the hotel was full of loose women. He had heard about my stay in the Castle and he let me know it would not do to have that reputation in Uganda. I remember trying to explain the circumstances, but he left before I finished.

The next day found me on the road, bleary eyed and feeling distinctly queasy, heading for the dangerous tea growing areas.

Chapter 8 Working the Fields

After a harmless, uneventful drive along the shores of Lake Victoria and then on into the foothills of the Mountains of the Moon, I drove to the Namingomba Tea Estate. It was owned by Derek Broadhead-Williams, an old friend of Peter Winch's, and I was expected.

I was taken to my bungalow, on the top of a steep slope, with densely packed tea bushes brushing up against the side of the porch. I was further told that my day started at 5 A.M. at labor lines.

Labor lines was the morning roll call for the labor force that picked and made the tea. Rather like an army muster roll, the names of the laborers were called out and they answered "Aya" or "Dio" and were marked present. Then the division was made between the field crew, who picked the tea, and the tea makers, who worked in the factory.

My first week was spent working the fields, seeing how tea was picked, collected, and weighed. Making tea is a business. Tea estates are supposed to make money, and the green leaf is the beginning of the process. Green leaf is laden with moisture; it is very heavy, but it must be weighed. The pickers are paid based on how much they pick, so they were very conscious of the weight. Some would happily add stones, or the odd rock or two, and it was my job to make sure that what was weighed was all green leaf.

A normal day's work was about sixty kilos, or roughly 120 pounds of leaf. This is a lot. I tried my hand at picking and it was

The characteristic "two leaves and bud."

hard work. The wicker basket was heavy and hurt my head; the two leaves and a bud, far from being easy to pick, were so supple they were difficult to snap. The bushes were so dense that it was tough to force your way through them. After I'd collected half a basket, I handed the job back to the field supervisor, who had been watching me with an amused grin on his face. I headed back to the shade, suitably humbled.

In the field I learned how to get downwind of fertilizer applications, and to wear boots in the long grass. This was after I felt a funny feeling on my legs one morning—a kind of itchy, slimy feeling. Looking down, I saw little curly animals crawling up my legs—funny little things—and as they got higher, they got fatter. Leeches! Prancing around, I tore off my trousers and, naked from the waist down and surrounded by a laughing crew of pickers, I plucked off the leeches, ripping my skin on each one but not caring.

All the pluckers were male; that is one of the oddities of the estate world. In Asia, all the pluckers are women; in Africa, they are all men. I was in good company, and thereafter always wore boots

Boots were also pretty useful to protect against the snakes that occasionally would lie and bask on the dry, exposed roots, coiled and relaxed until you stepped on them. The comfortable feeling of boot leather up around your ankles was welcome.

The teas grown in Uganda were medium-grown. They were not prized for their extraordinary flavor but more for their color and strength. They were manufactured to accentuate these characteristics.

The classic way of making tea is to roll the tea leaves after they have withered and the natural moisture has been reduced to about forty percent of what it was on the bush. At that point, it is pliable and can be rolled to a tight twist, which is the classic pekoe tea.

If the pekoe broke during rolling, it was sifted out and became broken pekoe tea. If it broke yet again during rolling, it became quite small and fell to the floor. At that point, it was collected by the tea makers by waving fans at the tea and collecting it all in a corner; this tea was called fannings tea, or broken pekoe fannings. Anything smaller than fannings was called a dust, for obvious reasons, but was still collected and sold.

These are the primary grades of pekoe tea—pekoe, broken pekoe, fannings, and dust. You can see that these grades all relate to size, and not taste, although the smaller the leaf, the stronger the taste. Dust, therefore, is always much stronger than broken pekoe from the same estate.

When it came my time to serve in the Namingomba factory, I was entranced by the rich, vegetative smell that permeated the building; it was fresh and juicy and smells healthy.

The leaf came in from the field, was carefully weighed, and then weighed again because it had already started to lose moisture. It was placed in long troughs with chicken wire at a depth of three feet; cool or warm air was then blown through the troughs and up through the leaves to control the pace of the "withering."

In the old days in Ceylon and India, they used to place the freshly picked tea leaves on multiple racks in the lofts above the tea machinery. These lofts were surrounded by hundreds of windows, which were opened to breezes that would naturally wither the leaves. This system took up to seventeen hours to complete.

TEA TALES

The traditional way of making black tea is to roll the tea a number of times—anywhere from four to six times. At the end of each roll, the leaf is collected and allowed to ferment (or oxidise) for an hour of two. You thus end up with different sizes of tea leaves called "grades." After fermentation, the various grades are dried in an oven. After drying, which lowers the moisture content of the leaf down to about two percent, the tea is sifted to make sure the right grades are packed into foil-lined chests—or nowadays, multi-walled, foil-lined paper sacks—and sent off to the nearest auction center.

This way of making tea is called "orthodox" manufacture and is by far the slowest and most gentle method of making tea. It is so gentle, in fact, that the fine hairs that are on some of the tea bushes are not removed during the processing. When the tea is dried, the hairs turn a golden color. This type of tea leaf is called "flowery" because of its style and "tippy" because of the fine hairs. If the color of the hair after drying is gold, it is called "golden."

But there is another method of making black tea. It is violent, fast, and very effective, producing a lot of tea very quickly that tastes similar. This method is called "cut, tear, and crush" (CTC). I also have heard it called "cut, tear, and curl," but to be honest, I do not see where any curling could take place.

The beauty of the orthodox method is that it produces lots of different sizes of tea and lots of different tastes. Orthodox teas can be graduated into many grades and sub-grades. Not so with CTC. This method is efficient. With CTC, about 80 percent of the leaf ends up as one grade: pekoe fannings. It is even, small, and brews up with great color and intensity. The other 20 percent of the CTC manufacture is split between broken pekoe and dust.

A factory in Ceylon (Sri Lanka) with "withering lofts" up top for drying tea.

This accounts for tea factories in India and Ceylon being built on top of ridges, to catch all the breeze that was available.

It also meant that tea factories were very imposing buildings, masses of shuttered windows, painted white; they lorded it over the surrounding valleys. You get the sense, as you drive up the winding roads to the factory, that you were meant to feel small and insignificant—a lot like the cathedrals in the Middle Ages, or perhaps buildings in Communist China. Huge buildings designed to make mortal man feel mortal.

Once the leaf had been withered it was taken by conveyor belt directly to the rotorvane machine. The rotorvane was essentially a huge sausage maker; you fed the leaf in at one end and a spiral feed took the leaf up through a tube, crushing it as it went, so it popped out at the end in a semi-macerated state.

The leaf was then fed directly into the CTC machine. This machine consisted of two rollers with razor-sharp ridges running vertically, so that they interlocked. The leaf pieces, already chopped up by the rotorvane, would fall into the CTC rollers and come out the other side in a stream of shredded tea.

Most factories had a bank of three to four CTC machines. Namingomba had three, and after going through all three the leaf had been reduced in size to something resembling a pinhead. All of this processing would take ninety seconds from the first CTC cut to the last. The macerated leaf was then fermented in trays and dried in a wood-fired dryer.

This last item was a monster and had two issues. The first was that it required a lot of wood to keep it fired up, and the second was that if it leaked smoke into the drying chambers, the tea took on a smoky taste that ruined its value. Part of my task in the factory was to check the dryer for leaks.

Seeing as the temperature was always set at about 270 degrees Fahrenheit for the feeder mouth, this was hot, unpleasant, dusty work. But that's what trainees are kept on the estate to do, and I learnt to love the rhythm of the days, the cool nights, and the blinding hot dryer room. When it came time to leave the estate and get on the road to develop the trading business, I was filled with a sense of regret. The plantation life was one that appealed to me—I enjoyed the routine and the fresh air—but my future lay in a different direction.

Chapter 9
Ahead of His Time

In a land of eccentrics, Frazer Simpson was a leading light. He and his brother ran the Kijura tea estate. As an independent estate, it clearly was a sales opportunity for me. He quickly became a friend and the most entertaining of companions.

The Kijura estate was located in the foothills of the Mountains of the Moon. You reached it by a torturous road that was full of potholes and stones, and surrounded by tall grass so that you could not see around any corners. On my first visit to introduce myself I stayed in town, but was soon invited to stay at the estate the next time I was in the area.

The tea trade in those days included well-established companies such as Mitchell Cotts, which had large holdings that they would not let a trader near. Other estates were owned by Indian groups that were very suspicious of traders in any form. Finally, the independent estates were tea gardens that were hacked out of the virgin bush by intrepid settlers; these settlers raised their families and hopes of a better life.

Kijura was one such independent estate. Frazer was the younger brother, and he used to drive his elder brother John to distraction. Frazer liked to tinker and was constantly changing the parameters of the production in a never-ending attempt to improve the quality of the product. The trouble was that he changed not just one element at a time but many, so when he did produce a good batch of tea he did not know which change was the one that caused the improvement.

Dinner with the two of them was hysterical.

"Changed the withering temperature, I saw." That came from John.

"Yes, and added another six inches of leaf." That from Frazer

"Got a better wither?" from John.

"Yes, I think so." Frazer.

"What caused it?" John.

"Could have been the extra six inches, or the temperature change." Frazer.

My most memorable wakening was at 7 A.M. after a night of hospitality from the brothers. I awoke to Frazer pounding on my bedroom door.

"Barry, you must come. I've done it!"

I joined him moments later, boots on, shorts on, shirt going on, no need for a hat. When Frazer said he had "done it," best not to wait around and see what he had done.

His racket had awakened John, who emerged tousled and equally bleary-eyed.

"What's up?"

"I've done it. I've made a dramatic improvement." Frazer, when excited, tended to hop from foot to foot, going at it like a demented dervish.

"Stop hopping, Frazer, and tell me what you have done." John.

"Show you," and with that Frazer stopped hopping and shot out the door. We heard his jeep start up and roar off up the factory road.

"Better follow him; no idea what my bloody brother has done." John left to get his car keys and moments later we joined in the drive to the factory.

In the factory, sitting in the center of the fermenting room, was a refrigerated Coke machine with a power cord coming down from an electric light socket. The front of the Coke machine had been cut open, and a reed basket had been jammed in and stuffed with fermenting tea. A low hum came from the Coke machine.

"Chilled fermentation. That's the answer." Frazer resumed the dervish dance. "Come, Barry, taste it." He shot off into the tasting room where three teas had been prepared.

I tasted them. They were superb. Wonderful color, fabulous flavor, better than anything I had ever tasted from a Uganda tea estate.

I gave my professional opinion: "Wow," I said.

Frazer's hops elevated another inch or so. "Wow," he said. "Wow, I knew it. I knew it. It's the answer."

I tasted them. They were superb. Wonderful color, fabulous flavor, better than anything I had ever tasted from a Uganda tea estate.

John loomed in the doorway. "Frazer, how much tea does that Coke machine hold?"

"I don't know—couple of pounds."

"How much do we produce in a day?"

"About five thousand pounds, but I've thought this through. We need a large commercial refrigerator unit that we can run like a dryer, keep the teas in there for two hours, and then dry them."

John raised his eyes to the ceiling. "Frazer, do you know how much they cost to buy and to run? The electricity cost alone would break us."

Frazer stopped hopping. I felt he needed a boost.

"These are damned good teas, Frazer, really good." But I could see my word had not worked any magic.

Fifteen years later, I was touring a tea factory in Kenya. A large, elevated conveyor belt carried the CTC leaf and dropped it into a machine that had blowers running down its side, blasting cold air over the fermenting leaf, which was slowly moved from top to bottom.

"What's that?" I asked, knowing the answer before it came.

"That's the latest in chilled fermentation; the leaf has cold air blown on it. Produces very good liquors."

Somewhere in the universe I thought I heard the distinctive sound of someone hopping.

Chapter 10
Guns & Golf

LIFE IN UGANDA BECAME INCREASINGLY DANGEROUS. THE POLITICAL SITUATION WAS UNSTABLE AND IT BECAME SENSIBLE TO BE HOME EARLY RATHER THAN LATER. BUSINESS BEGAN TO SUFFER AS ONE OF MY PRIME ADVANTAGES BEGAN TO SLIP AWAY—TIME.

I had developed a system whereby I received samples and offers from estates like Kijura and Namingoba and offered contracts for them overseas via telex on a "subject to approval of sample basis." This meant that I had tasted the teas, they were okay, and if the buyer did not like the sample I sent him he could cancel the contract. All of this would take place as the teas were being packed on the estate or on their way to Kampala.

If I sold the tea before it got to Kampala, I was able to divert it to our warehouse, put it on a railway wagon, and send it directly to the ships in Mombasa. This procedure was saving a lot of money for everybody, and giving the estate a much higher return than they would receive from going to auction in Mombasa with all its fees, or even worse, being sent all the way to the UK to go to auction there.

But with the advent of the security situation, samples began to take longer and longer to get to me, and even my trips to the estates became more and more risky. It was clear that the country was coming to a boil. One evening I was stopped, while returning to Kampala after my twice-monthly visit to the tea estates nestled up against the Mountains of the Moon.

It had been a normal day when I left Fort Portal, slightly hung over from an evening with two local planters. The drive had been uneventful until I had rounded the corner and been pulled up by the crude roadblock. Chairs, a sofa, and an upended table had stopped me. I was the only car at the block; in fact, I was the only car on the road that I could see.

Six soldiers manned the roadblock. All of them had their eyes on me, their guns loosely pointed in my direction. What I did not know was that someone had tried to assassinate Milton Obote, the president of Uganda, and a curfew had been imposed. I had been on the road and had not heard the news.

The short, stubby snout of the machine gun was about six inches from my face and looked like a railway tunnel.

"What are you doing here?" The sergeant's voice was harsh and demanding.

"I am driving to Kampala," I replied, keeping both hands on the steering wheel to stop them from shaking.

"Where are you coming from? What are you doing here?"

"I came from Fort Portal. I am tea taster." I looked up into the eyes of the sergeant holding the gun, trying to connect, trying to make myself human to him.

"A what?" The gun jerked toward my ear.

"A tea taster." It seemed an absurd thing to say while staring at the mouth of a machine gun.

"What is in those bags in the back seat?" The gun gestured over my shoulder.

"They are tea samples."

"Tea samples? What are you doing with tea samples?"

"I was up in Fort Portal collecting tea samples. I buy and sell tea." I stopped talking.

The gun moved back a fraction. I sat still. Uganda in 1969 was no place to be. Two years away from the coup run by Idi Amin, it was a seething ferment of suppression and violence. I had been in Uganda for two years. Twice a month I would take the six-hour drive up to Fort Portal, collect the tea samples, drive around and visit the estates, have a game or two of golf and dinner at the club, and then head back to Kampala. My treasure trove of fresh tea samples sat on my rear seat, well away from the gasoline fumes in the trunk.

The gun by my face did not waver. "What do you have in the back of the car?"

"My suitcase and my golf clubs."

The gun snapped back into my face. "Clubs." The voice rose. "What clubs?"

I was stumped. How do you explain golf to someone who does not know the game? I looked up into the sergeant's eyes again.What I saw scared me. I was raised in Africa and I knew the signs of anger, remorse and, worst of all, panic. What I saw was panic.

"Can I get out of the car and show you?"

The sergeant stepped back and I opened the door; the rifles suddenly swiveled in tight hands and pointed directly at me. I shut off the car engine, took the keys, ever so carefully walked around to the trunk and opened it, and then stepped back. The sergeant advanced cautiously and peered into the back.

LOCAL LORE

Of all of the oppressive regimes in African history—and there have been a lot of them—Idi Amin's is considered to be one of the worst. During his 8-year reign he is rumored to have tortured and killed close to 500,000 of his fellow Ugandans.

Notoriously paranoid and prone to "visions," some speculate that his erratic behavior may have been due to late stage syphilis. It's certainly true that he acted strangely. At one point he declared himself King of Scotland, and at his death his most popular title was "His Excellency President for Life, Field Marshal Al Hadji Doctor Idi Amin, VC, DSO, MC, Lord of All the Beasts of the Earth and Fishes of the Sea, and Conqueror of the British Empire in Africa in General and Uganda in Particular."

Suddenly "Tea Master" doesn't sound quite so impressive.

My suitcase was resting on top of my golf bag. The sergeant gestured to me to remove the suitcase. I pulled it out and lay it on the ground. The sergeant looked at the golf bag and gestured at it.

I reached in and pulled a golf tee from the little fastener on the outside of the bag, and held it up for him to see. He reached out and touched it, then replaced his hand on the gun barrel. I took that as a good sign and pulled out a brand-new Dunlop golf ball and peeled away the wrapper. He reached forward and fondled the ball for a moment, then stepped back.

I looked in his eyes. The panic had gone and curiosity was creeping in. I held out the tee and ball and walked over to the grassy edge of the road. I stuck the tee in the ground, placed the ball on top, and stepped back, terribly conscious of the rifles concentrated on my back.

The sergeant looked at me. I walked back to the trunk and ever so slowly pulled out my driver. I looked at the sergeant and at the leveled gun, which had now moved up to my chest, and nodded at the golf ball.

He stepped back and I walked over and faced into the jungle. I addressed the ball and took a swing at it, knocking it way off into the trees. I turned and watched a broad smile break across the sergeant's face.

The sergeant reached up and removed his gun sling, handed the gun to the nearest soldier, and reached for the driver.

"Ball," he said, nodding at the golf bag.

I watched him smack the ball off into the jungle and then roar with laughter. That was that. Every soldier had a swing with the driver until I had no golf balls left. The soldiers waved me on my way, with the advice to get off the road as soon as possible because a curfew had been declared.

As I drove away I started to breathe again and wonder at the reality that was Africa. I could easily have died that day; instead, I made some friends and I am sure they told the story of the mad Englishman and his golf clubs. But what if my life had ended there? And what on earth had led me, a tea taster, to be in harm's way? I decided that it was time to move on. Africa had my heart, but the next stop on my journey would be elsewhere.

Dear Reader,

I hope you've enjoyed this excerpt from my book. I think it is always easy to write about something you love. I love tea and the world of tea. I love the life it has given me, the adventures it offers me, and the challenges it continues to present. I am sure this love shines through on the preceding pages and I trust I've imparted some of it to you.

If you enjoyed the early days of my life in tea and would like to know what happened next, log onto www.CooperTea.com for information on the book from which this excerpt was taken."

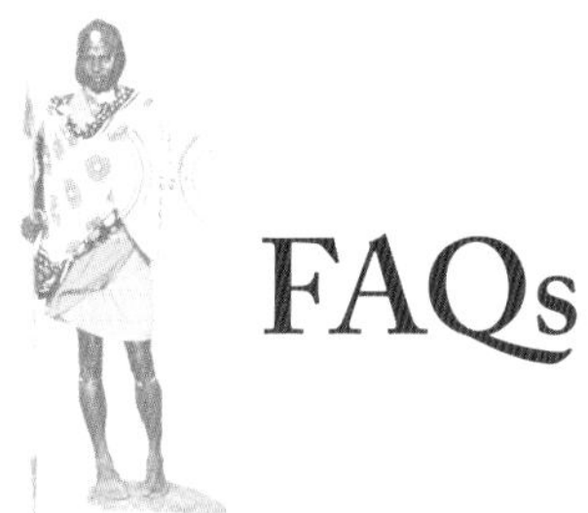

FAQs

HERE'S A SHORT LIST OF ANSWERS TO FREQUENTLY ASKED QUESTIONS (FAQs) I HAVE ANSWERED OVER THE YEARS.

Q. What are you doing these days?

A. Well, actually, I spend my days finding new and better ways to bring good tea to people.

I began by developing a new and better way of brewing tea: the tea pod. In the interest of full disclosure, I must add that I own the worldwide rights to the tea pod, so I do have a vested interest in seeing this method of brewing tea succeed. The patent was granted in the US in 1999 and around the world thereafter.

The idea for the tea pod came to me in 1998 when I was sitting in a coffeehouse watching espresso coffee being made. I wondered how tea would behave under that kind of heat and pressure. I purchased a little espresso machine, made up some pods, and was amazed at how quickly the tea was made and how good it tasted.

When I discovered that my invention made a glass of iced tea in 35 seconds as well, I realized I really did have a good idea and applied for a patent. My patent was granted immediately with all claims—meaning the tea pod was a unique and different idea.

The problem with iced tea is that it usually takes an age to make. You have to boil the water, infuse the tea bags, create a concentrate, dilute the concentrate, put the concentrate in the refrigerator, and then wait for it to chill down. It makes no sense not to brew anything less than a full pitcher of tea.

Not so with the pod. In 35 seconds, you can brew a glass of black tea; in another 35 seconds, a glass of green tea; and in another 35 seconds, a cup of hot herbal tea. So in under 2 minutes, you can have three perfectly made, and very good, teas—with no pitcher taking up a lot of space in the refrigerator.

The truth is, the tea pod is a better way of making tea. It is faster and more consistent, and it extracts more tea solids and antioxidants from tea in 35 seconds than a 3-minute traditional brew.

The next thing I tackled was fountain tea. 7-Eleven, a convenience store company known to try new and different products, asked me if I could develop a bag-in-the-box (BIB) concentrate that could be served on the fountain—and taste good.

BIB tea comes out of the fountain just like Coke or Pepsi. It is a tea concentrate that is mixed with water and served through the fountain dispenser. The setup is very simple. The bag has a valve that is hooked onto a line that sucks out the concentrate at a ratio of 5:1 or 7:1 (1 part of concentrate to 5 parts or 7 parts of water).

The difference between my product and the marketplace is that my unsweetened version is 100 percent natural—no chemicals, no additives, just tea and water.

Compare this to the leading national brands: They have upward of 20 ingredients combined in their BIB products, including artificial flavors and red dyes. Of course, you can't read an ingredient list on a fountain dispenser or in a restaurant. You can only taste the product. Mine tastes like real tea; it is as simple as that. It tastes like real tea because it is real tea.

Most recently, I've turned my attention to a line of ready-to-drink bottled teas. Once again, they are made from real tea, and you can taste the difference. I've also introduced a line of high-energy teas. They possess all the concentrated energy of other high-energy drinks, but they are made with real tea. So, you also get a healthy dose of antioxidants and vitamins. Recognizing that sometimes folks need an extra boost of energy, I figured it was about time someone came up with one that contains some stuff that's good for you—and actually tastes good.

Q: What is your favorite tea?

A: I have many favorites. That is the beauty of tea, there are so many to choose from. However, I have put together my "Dream Blend." It consisted of high-grown Nuwara Eliyas' picked in May, Kenya tea picked east of the Great Rift Valley, a high grown Rwandan valley tea for its earthy taste, and finally, just a touch of second flush Darjeeling to give it a little bite. Of course this is an impossible blend to market commercially. Such teas are not available in sufficient quantities to assure a year round consistent tea. It was one helluva blend though! Knocked your socks off!

Q: How many different types of tea are there?

A: Thousands.

Q: Can I reuse a tea bag?

A: Never dry out a tea bag and reuse it. Why would you want to reuse a tea bag?

Q. Is Green Tea better for you than Black Tea?

A: It comes from the same bush, only the processing is different. So ignoring the issues of origin, elevation and season, Black Tea actually has as much goodness as Green Tea. Most people just don't know it.

Q: How much Green Tea does the world produce?

A: Almost 676,000 metric tons.

Q: Who drinks the most Green Tea?

A: The Chinese.

Q: Can I drink Green Tea with milk?

A: No, no, no, never drink green tea with milk!

Q: What is Earl Grey?

A: Earl Grey is normally a black tea from China that also contains the oil from a little, pear-shaped orange called the bergamot orange, added to it for flavor.

Q: Should I add milk to Earl Grey Tea?

A: Never add milk to a good Earl Grey. Add milk to a poor Earl Grey, but it won't make much difference.

Q: Does tea have more caffeine than coffee?

A: Yes.

Q: But it says on the boxes that it had less caffeine than coffee.

A: Well that's because it takes 200 cups of tea from 1 pound and you can only make 50 cups of coffee from 1 pound. But on a pound for pound basis, tea in its natural state has more caffeine than coffee. All clear?

No? Okay, well, on a cup-to-cup basis, tea has less caffeine than coffee does. Okay?

Q: What is the most expensive tea in the world?

A: White tea from China.

Q: What is the cheapest tea in the world?

A: Burma, Georgia, Iran and Turkey have produced some pretty rough stuff over the years.

Q: Georgia, U.S.A.?

A: No, Georgia that used to be part of Russia.

Q: Does the United States produce any tea?

A: Yes. There is a plantation down in South Carolina owned by the royal family of tea, David and Eunice Bigelow. It can truly claim to be the only tea grown in America.

Q: What is the rarest tea in the world?

A: Probably the only tea grown in America.

Q: How did you become a tea taster?

A: Luck.

Q: What do you do with all the tea you have to taste?

A: I spit it into a spittoon. Ugh! Agreed.

Q: How many cups of tea do you drink a day?

A: On the average, about six.

Q: What advice would you give a trainee tea taster?

A: Wear boots in the tea fields because you cannot see the snakes when you walk among the bushes.

Q: How should I store tea?

A: In an airtight container in a cupboard away from the light and away from spices. A glass jar will do, as long as it has a lid.

Q: Who drinks the strongest tea in the world?

A: I think the Irish.

Q: Who drinks the weakest tea in the world?

A: Don't know, but Americans who dip their tea bags into a cup of hot water for about 10 seconds have to come close.

Q: Who produces the most tea in the world?

A: China. The experts may say India, but China produces a lot of tea that never reaches any sort of market as it is made and consumed by the very people who grow it.

Q: Who produces the least?

A: The USA.

Q: Which country drinks the most tea per person?

A: The Republic of Ireland. The Irish drink about 2.70 kilos of tea a year (that's about 6 lbs of tea per person, including women and children). Lets hear it for the Irish!

Q: What is the consumption in the USA?

A: Less than three quarters of a pound per person per year.

Q: What does CTC mean?

A: Cut, Tear and Curl. It refers to a method of manufacturing tea.

Q: What is "Cut Pekoe Black Tea"?

A: It is the Pekoe grade of tea that's been cut to fit into a tea bag.

Q: Does "Cut Pekoe Black Tea" mean it is good tea?

A: No.

Q: How much tea is produced in the whole world?

A: Approximately 3,000,0000 metric tons of tea a year.

Q: How many cups is that?

A: You do the math. Multiply the tons by 2,000. Then multiply that result by 2.2046. Then divide that result by 2.2. That will give you 2,727,272,728 cups.

Q: Will the world ever run out of Tea?

A: No

Q: What is "Instant Tea"?

A: It is tea that has been brewed in a giant kettle, the components extracted, mixed together and then spray dried into a powder.

Q: Has anything in tea ever been found to be bad for you?

A: Not to my knowledge. There is always the debate about caffeine, but as coffee and most soft drinks are loaded with the stuff, it seems a silly debate to me.

Q: How long does Tea last in a box on the grocery shelf?

A: About 2 years.

Q: How long in a pantry?

A: In a sealed container that is airtight, about six months.

Longer if you don't mind the quality going "off" a bit. By "off a bit," I mean stale.

Q: Which is better to brew: loose tea, tea pods or tea bags?

A: It all depends on what you are looking for. For a cultural experience that's elegant, time bound and leaves gaps for conversation and polite exchanges, nothing beats loose tea. However, if you want some convenience and a dangling string and tag along with a dripping tea bag to get rid off, nothing beats a tea bag.

If you want speed, convenience, neatness and a great cup or glass of tea, then nothing beats a tea pod.

Q: What is a tea brick?

A: It is an ancient form of tea and currency. The Chinese made tea into bricks, loaded them aboard camel trains and trekked them over to Russia. They were then sold or exchanged for goods and broken up and brewed. It boggles the mind that anything that had been bounced along the sides of a sweating camel for months on end would taste anything but awful, but there you go, there is no accounting for taste. (Refer back to the least expensive tea in the world.)

Q: How do I contact you?

A: E-mail me at bcooper@coopertea.com and I will answer any further questions you may have. Or you can visit my website at www.coopertea.com.

Index

Index